WORLD WAR I AFTERMATH

Essential Library

An Imprint of Abdo Publishing
abdopublishing.com

ESSENTIAL LIBRARY OF

WORLD WAR I

BY TOM STREISSGUTH

abdopublishing.com

Published by Abdo Publishing, a division of ABDO, PO Box 398166, Minneapolis, Minnesota 55439. Copyright © 2016 by Abdo Consulting Group, Inc. International copyrights reserved in all countries. No part of this book may be reproduced in any form without written permission from the publisher. Essential Library™ is a trademark and logo of Abdo Publishing.

Printed in the United States of America, North Mankato, Minnesota

092015
012016

THIS BOOK CONTAINS
RECYCLED MATERIALS

Cover Photo: Bettmann/Corbis/AP Images
Interior Photos: Bettmann/Corbis/AP Images, 1; Uhrig/Picture-Alliance/DPA/AP Images, 4; DPA/Picture-Alliance/DPA/AP Images, 7, 87; AP Images, 9, 38, 45, 56, 59, 63, 71, 81, 99 (left); Library of Congress, 11, 41; World History Archive/Newscom, 13, 21, 37, 50, 98 (right); Virginia Mayo/AP Images, 15; JT Vintage/ZumaPress/Newscom, 16; SuperStock/Glow Images, 19, 99 (right); Red Line Editorial, 25; Mirrorpix/Newscom, 26; akg-images/Newscom, 29, 31; Staff/Mirrorpix/Newscom, 35; Everett Collection/Newscom, 48, 84; Bain News Service/Library of Congress, 54; Bettmann/Corbis, 60, 75; STR/Keystone/Corbis, 67; Everett Historical/Shutterstock Images, 68, 79, 83; National Library of Medicine/KRT/Newscom, 72; Berliner Verlag/Archiv/Picture-Alliance/DPA/AP Images, 89; Antique Research Centre/AGF RM/Glow Images, 92; DPA Dena/Picture-Alliance/DPA/AP Images, 95, 98 (left)

Editor: Nick Rebman
Series Designers: Kelsey Oseid and Maggie Villaume

Library of Congress Control Number: 2015945646

Cataloging-in-Publication Data

Streissguth, Tom.
 World War I aftermath / Tom Streissguth.
  p. cm. -- (Essential library of World War I)
ISBN 978-1-62403-926-3 (lib. bdg.)
Includes bibliographical references and index.
1. World War, 1914-1918--Juvenile literature.   I. Title.
940.4/21--dc23

2015945646

CONTENTS

Croisilles, a town in northern France, lies in ruins after a battle.

SPRING OFFENSIVE, FALL ARMISTICE

By the spring of 1918, World War I had been in progress for nearly four years. Over that time, the Allied armies of France and the United Kingdom had reached a stalemate with Germany. The western front that stretched across northern France and western Belgium had become a killing field. Millions of men had fought and died for little gain in territory or strategic advantage.

To break the standoff, Germany's military leader General Erich Ludendorff ordered an all-out offensive west of the French city of Cambrai. The German units would stage an assault against the British Fifth Army, to begin at dawn on March 21, 1918. With American reinforcements arriving in Europe soon to assist the

Allies, the German leaders wanted a victory on the battlefield as soon as possible to force the British and French to accept a cease-fire.

The Spring Offensive began with a massive artillery bombardment. The Germans opened up with 6,500 heavy guns and mortars, firing 1.2 million shells at the Allied lines in a span of five hours.[1] Germany's Eighteenth Army advanced, reaching the outskirts of Amiens and the town of Albert. From the front, long-range German guns could now bombard civilians in the capital of Paris.

But General Ludendorff had ordered his troops to advance at all possible speed, bringing minimal equipment and food. This extended the German supply lines, preventing crucial resupply of the frontline units. When the hungry German infantrymen reached French towns, they stopped advancing and began looting. This stopped the Spring Offensive in its tracks, just as the first American troops were arriving in France.

In July, Ludendorff sent 52 divisions against Allied positions around the city of Reims, northeast of Paris.[2] French and American armies, including the US Third Infantry Division, stopped the offensive in three days. Ludendorff and his aides realized Germany could no longer resupply its army at the same rate it was losing troops, ammunition, and equipment. Through the summer of 1918, Germany's military situation grew even worse. British and American units were now forcing the German troops from positions they had been holding for the last four years.

General Erich Ludendorff, *right*, studies a map with General Field Marshal Paul von Hindenburg, *left*, and Kaiser Wilhelm II, *center*.

With the failure of the Spring Offensive, and the setbacks of the following summer, Ludendorff knew Germany was beaten. In late September, he informed Kaiser Wilhelm II, the German emperor, that the army faced a hopeless situation on the western front. Although Germany could probably stop an invasion of its homeland, morale was sinking fast. German troops were at the point of mutiny. Thousands of men were deserting the front lines, and risking a firing squad, to return home.

PRESIDENT WILSON AND THE PEACE

Elected president of the United States in 1912, Woodrow Wilson had kept his country out of the conflict when it began in 1914. But the American public followed the war closely in newspapers, which featured front-page reports of German atrocities in Belgium. In 1915, a German submarine sank the RMS *Lusitania*, and 128 American civilians died.[3] After Wilson's reelection in 1916, American opinion began to turn. In April 1917, Wilson asked Congress for a declaration of war. Congress agreed, and American troops began landing in Europe later that year.

Wilson believed the end of the war, when it came, should bring a new era of peace based on several important principles. He laid out these ideas, known as the Fourteen Points, in a speech to Congress in January 1918. That fall, German leaders saw the Fourteen Points as the basis for an armistice with the Allies.

The United Kingdom and France had been fighting for more than four years. They had expended huge sums on the war and suffered nearly 10 million military casualties.[4] Trench warfare and artillery bombardments had devastated the

Woodrow Wilson reads the Fourteen Points to Congress.

plains of Belgium and northern France. British and French leaders wanted no less than an unconditional surrender by Germany.

Wilson insisted the Allies accept Germany's offer. Otherwise, he promised, the United States would negotiate a separate peace with Germany. He also insisted that Wilhelm II, the emperor of Germany, must abdicate, or give up power.

France and the United Kingdom were not prepared to carry on without American help. On November 9, Germany announced that Wilhelm had given up his throne. Two days later, Germany, France, and the United Kingdom signed the armistice ending the war in western Europe. Germany was to retreat immediately from France and Belgium, allow Allied troops to occupy three cities on Germany's side of the Rhine River, and submit to other severe terms.

HARSH TERMS AT VERSAILLES

The Allies threatened to resume the war if Germany should take any hostile actions or break the terms of the armistice. The leaders of the United Kingdom, France, the United States, and Italy agreed to meet in Versailles, near the French capital of Paris. They would draw up an agreement formally ending the war and setting permanent terms of the peace on Germany.

SUBMARINED INTO WAR

The sinking of the *Lusitania* was only one of many incidents that led to American involvement in World War I. In the spring of 1916, after a German submarine sank the unarmed French ship *Sussex*, Woodrow Wilson threatened to cut off all diplomatic ties with Germany. The result was the Sussex Pledge in May 1916. Germany agreed that U-boats would not attack any passenger ships or ships of neutral countries. U-boat captains would also allow crews of enemy merchant ships to abandon their vessels before an attack.

As the war dragged on without result, however, German naval commanders came to believe open submarine warfare was the way to victory. After all, the United States was already supplying arms to Germany's enemies, which made the United States, in effect, an enemy combatant. A few sinkings might even end the war before the Americans could send troops across the Atlantic.

In January, Germany declared its intention to resume unrestricted submarine warfare, and by the end of March 1917, U-boats had sent several American ships to the bottom of the Atlantic Ocean. For Wilson, this was the last straw that would make the president break his own pledge of neutrality in the war.

WOODROW WILSON
1856–1924

Running on the slogan "He kept us out of war," Woodrow Wilson was reelected president of the United States in 1916.[5] But within six months, he had brought the United States into World War I on the side of the Allies.

Wilson emerged as the global political hero of World War I. But as the Europeans hailed his accomplishment, Wilson came to believe he did not need to compromise—with Germany, with the Allies, or with the opposing political party at home. Wilson, a Democrat, appointed no Republicans to the Versailles peace commission. He tolerated no opposition to the League of Nations, the newly formed international organization dedicated to world peace, among the leaders of the United Kingdom and France. And he made no concessions to treaty opponents in Congress, insisting the document be ratified just as he had negotiated it.

As a result, the treaty was defeated in Congress. Opposing politicians believed it would set the United States up for dangerous entanglements in future European troubles. Bitter and disappointed, Wilson suffered declining health and in the last months of his presidency became bedridden.

The Treaty of Versailles was signed in January 1919. For Germany, the terms were harsh. Germany had to surrender Alsace-Lorraine, a long-contested region along the border between France and Germany. Germany also had to give up significant portions of its eastern territory. In addition, Germany was to have no military presence at all in the Rhineland, the country's industrial heartland. The Allies would occupy this region to prevent any future German attacks on France or Belgium. Germany had to disband its air force and scrap its submarine fleet. The treaty also limited the German army to 100,000 men.[6]

WILSON'S OPPONENTS AT HOME

Although he won two terms as president, Woodrow Wilson did not enjoy universal support for his foreign policy. His opponents in the Republican Party did not want the United States further entangling itself in European affairs, or trying to impose high-minded philosophical notions on a continent that seemed eternally at war. President Theodore Roosevelt, who served two terms before Wilson's time in office, was not a fan of Wilson or the Treaty of Versailles. Although Roosevelt supported the use of American military and economic power around the world, he was suspicious of Wilson's idealism and did not want the United States getting tangled in European conflicts. He had this to say about Wilson's efforts:

Our allies, and our enemies, and Woodrow Wilson himself should all understand that Mr. Wilson has no authority whatever to speak for the American people at this time. His leadership and the Fourteen Points and his four supplementary points and his five complementary points and all his utterances every which way have ceased to have any shadow of right to be accepted as expressive of the will of the American people.[7]

World leaders gathered to negotiate the Treaty of Versailles.

It was not just the loss of territory or the dismantling of its military that weighed the most on Germany. Instead, the biggest outrage, in the minds of many German citizens, was Article 231. This "war guilt" clause placed blame for the war squarely on Germany.[8] It also formed the basis of the demand for reparations—payments Germany must make to the Allied governments for war damages.

Germans believed they were wrongly blamed, however. The war had started with the mobilization of Austria-Hungary against Serbia. Austria-Hungary had then called on Germany to come to its aid; these two countries became known as the Central powers. The Austro-Hungarian government believed it would have to also fight Russia, an ally of Serbia.

The war guilt clause recognized none of this history and treated the war as if its only cause was Germany's invasion of Belgium and France. Ultimately, resentment of the Versailles treaty would play an important role in the rise of a new, even more belligerent German government in the 1930s.

SURVEYING THE DAMAGE

The war had resulted in the deaths of approximately 15 million civilians and soldiers on all sides. There were approximately 8.5 million battle deaths and 21.2 million wounded out of 65 million men mobilized for the war.[9] According to an estimate by the United Kingdom's National Archives, the total cost of the war to all sides was $208 billion.[10] The cost was $32 billion to the United States alone.[11]

JAPAN AND WORLD WAR I

Japan had entered World War I on the side of the Allies. Japanese representatives also signed the Versailles treaty of 1919. The United Kingdom had enlisted the Japanese to attack German ships as well as Germany's possessions in Asia and the Pacific. By the Treaty of Versailles, Japan gained the former German colony of Shandong in China.

The war gave Japanese industries a boost, but a postwar recession led to the rise of a militant faction in the Japanese government. By the start of World War II (1939–1945), Japan was aggressively expanding in the Pacific region and preparing to confront its former allies in Europe and the United States.

The years of trench warfare devastated a long stretch of once-fertile farmland in northern France and southwestern Belgium. Trenches, bomb craters, and unexploded shells made even walking across the ground extremely dangerous.

Evidence of World War I, such as this German bunker, can still be found across southwestern Belgium and northern France.

Heavy bombardments and street fighting had destroyed hundreds of small towns as well as entire cities. In many places, poison gas had contaminated the natural environment.

It would take a generation for the region surrounding the western front to recover from the war. To this day, battlefield remains—including trench lines, tunnels, bunkers, concrete pillboxes, and barbed-wire supports—still litter the area. In addition, tens of thousands of soldiers remain where they fell, making the landscape in some places a vast cemetery of German, French, British, and American soldiers who never returned home.

Czar Nicholas II and his family were assassinated during the Russian Civil War, ending their dynasty.

CHAPTER

★ 2 ★

THE END OF EMPIRES

In 1914, Europe was still largely a continent of kingdoms and empires. Royal dynasties ruled Austria-Hungary, Russia, the Ottoman Empire, and Germany. The United Kingdom was ruled by a royal dynasty as well, though the British Parliament placed a check on the king's power and had the authority to write and vote on legislation.

The war brought several of these dynasties to an end, starting with the Romanovs of Russia. The poor judgment of Russian leaders, particularly Czar Nicholas II, fed public discontent that erupted in revolution in 1917. The czar was forced to abdicate, and the Bolshevik faction of the Russian Social Democratic Labor Party, led by Vladimir Lenin, took power in October. Russia's new leaders, known as the Reds, still had a major fight on their hands against the White faction, which supported czarist rule. A civil war erupted, during which the czar and his entire family were assassinated.

THE FALL AND SURVIVAL OF THE ROMANOVS

The Romanov dynasty came to a violent end in 1918, when their Bolshevik captors murdered the czar and his entire family in the basement of a house in Yekaterinburg, in the Ural Mountains region of Russia. After this event, a legend spread about the czar's youngest daughter, Anastasia, who some believed had survived.

Although Anastasia died in Yekaterinburg, there were dozens of other related survivors, most of whom fled into exile during the Russian civil war. Grand Duchess Maria Vladimirovna, the great-great-granddaughter of Czar Alexander II, was born in Spain in 1953 and claims to be the legitimate head of the Romanov dynasty. In 2013, the head of the Russian Orthodox Church officially gave her the church's support. Although the modern Russian government allows Maria to visit whenever she likes, it shows no interest in welcoming the Romanov dynasty back to Russia.

The Bolsheviks saw World War I as a conflict among Europe's ruling classes, fought by exploiting the sacrifice of workers and peasants. Russia's new leaders had no interest in fighting Germany, a nation they believed was ripe for a socialist revolution of its own. In March 1918, Russia agreed to terms with the Central powers and signed the Treaty of Brest-Litovsk. The war between Germany and Russia on the eastern front came to an end.

THE FALL OF THE HAPSBURGS

The Hapsburgs of Austria-Hungary were the oldest dynasty in Europe. Their reign over central Europe and the Balkan Mountain region dated to the 1200s. Emperor Franz Joseph had led the

VLADIMIR LENIN

1870–1924

Born into a middle-class family in Simbirsk, Russia (now known as Ulyanovsk), Vladimir Lenin rose to leadership of the Bolshevik faction of the Russian Social Democratic Labor Party. After the establishment of a Bolshevik government in 1918, he led the Red forces against the Whites, who were fighting—with the help of troops from the United Kingdom, Japan, France, and the United States—for restoration of the czar.

In 1922, victory in the civil war put the Bolsheviks in firm control of the country, which became known as the Soviet Union. The same year, however, Lenin suffered two strokes that permanently disabled him. In a document known as the Testament, he criticized other Bolshevik leaders, including Joseph Stalin, for their drive for power and the danger this posed to Bolshevik party unity.

By this time, however, Lenin no longer held sway in Russia, although he was still honored as the leader of the Russian Revolution. On Lenin's death, a power struggle took place that saw Stalin emerge as the sole ruler of the Soviet Union. Stalin showed his regard for Lenin by ordering the older man's corpse embalmed and placed on permanent display in the Kremlin, the ancient fortification in Moscow that served as the new capital of the Soviet empire.

19

Austro-Hungarian charge against Serbia in 1914. As did his predecessors, Franz Joseph believed the Hapsburg dynasty provided the best form of government for the patchwork of nationalities—Czech, Slovak, Polish, and others—that resided within Austria-Hungary's borders. By making an example of the Serbs, therefore, the Hapsburgs would strengthen their own authority in central Europe.

But the Austro-Hungarian army was not equal to the task. In the contested mountainous regions of the Alps, Italian and Austro-Hungarian units fought to a draw. The Serbs also put up a convincing fight against an Austro-Hungarian invasion that began in the summer of 1914. Emperor Franz Joseph died in November 1916, and his grand-nephew Charles took the throne. Charles tried, and failed, to reach a separate peace with the Allies. By the fall of 1918, the Austro-Hungarian army was facing a military defeat.

The nationalities that had lived for centuries under Hapsburg rule began declaring independence. A group of Polish leaders announced an independent Poland on October 7. The Czechs followed with a similar declaration on October 29. At this time, the South Slavs, including Croats, Slovenes, and Serbs, were preparing for unification under a monarchy of their own.

Austria-Hungary agreed to an armistice on November 3. On November 11, Charles surrendered his authority over the empire, proclaiming:

Filled with an unalterable love for my peoples I will not, with my person, be a hindrance to their free development. . . . I relinquish every participation in the administration of the state.

May the German-Austrian people realize harmony from the new adjustment. The happiness of my peoples was my aim from the beginning. My warmest wishes are that an internal peace will be able to heal the wounds of this war.[1]

With those words, the Hapsburg dynasty, after more than seven centuries in power, passed into history. The German-speaking provinces declared a Republic of Austria. A communist

Emperor Franz Joseph reigned from 1848 to 1916.

government ruled Hungary for three months before an invasion by Romania overthrew the Hungarian Soviet Republic in August 1919; after that, the country became known as the Kingdom of Hungary. In what had once been the empire's Balkan provinces, the Kingdom of Serbs, Croats, and Slovenes was born. This country later took the name of Yugoslavia.

THE OTTOMAN EMPIRE AND THE TURKISH REPUBLIC

In October 1918, the Armistice of Mudros ended the conflict between the Allies and the Ottoman Empire. The Ottoman sultans had ruled territory in southeastern Europe, Mesopotamia, and the Levant. But the Young Turk movement had forced the sultan to accept a constitution and representative government in 1908. Sultan Mehmed VI, who assumed his title earlier in 1918, was a mere figurehead.

The Allies occupied Istanbul, which had been the capital of the dynasty of the Ottoman Turks since the 1500s. British armies held Ottoman territory in Palestine, Syria, and Mesopotamia, including the major cities of Jerusalem,

CONFUSION IN SOUTH TYROL

During World War I, Austro-Hungarian and Italian troops fought and died in the mountainous region of South Tyrol. By the terms of the peace, South Tyrol joined Italy, although ethnic Germans remained in the majority. Under the rule of Benito Mussolini in the 1920s, Italy sent settlers to the region in an attempt to integrate South Tyrol into Italian society and culture, but the effort largely failed. South Tyrol is still divided between German and Italian speakers, and a political movement is pushing for independence from Italy and reunification with Austria.

Damascus, and Baghdad. The Allies imposed the Treaty of Sevres in August 1920, officially stripping the Ottoman realm of these possessions.

Turkish nationalists expelled the Allies from Istanbul and established a Turkish republic in 1922. On November 1, the new assembly proclaimed an end to the sultanate. Mehmed VI escaped on a British vessel to the island of Malta in the Mediterranean Sea. Under the leadership of war hero Mustafa Kemal, the Turks built a new state that was not under the control or influence of religious belief.

GENOCIDE IN ANATOLIA

A bitter political and cultural rivalry had existed for centuries between the Muslim Turks and the Christian Armenians, who lived in the eastern reaches of Anatolia. Armenians had long lived as second-class citizens within the Ottoman Empire. The Ottoman government suspected them of working with the Russians to weaken the empire's hold on the mountainous region.

During World War I, the Ottoman government joined the Central powers of Germany and Austria-Hungary, who were fighting against Russia. For the leaders of the sultanate, the war presented an opportunity to settle the Armenian question once and for all.

The Ottoman army swept into eastern Turkey to uproot Armenians and drive them from their homes. Massacres took place in hundreds of towns and villages. By the millions, the Armenians were marched into the arid deserts of Mesopotamia without food, water, or medicine. The final death toll reached at least 600,000, and some estimates raise the number of deaths to 1.3 million.[2] For the Turkish government, which still bans all discussion of the Armenian genocide in the media, the event remains a sore point to the present day.

The Turkish possessions on the European continent shrank to a sliver of land between Bulgaria and the Sea of Marmara. On the Asian continent, the republic controlled only the region of Anatolia, the ancient homeland of the Turks. The rest of the Ottoman Empire fell into the hands of the Allies.

A NEW MAP OF THE MIDDLE EAST

By the secret Sykes-Picot agreement of 1916, the United Kingdom and France agreed to share control of the region; the areas they controlled were known as mandates. The French controlled what later became Syria and Lebanon, while the British ruled over what was later Israel, the Palestinian territories, and Jordan. In November 1917, Arthur Balfour, the British foreign minister, had also agreed to reserve Palestine as a Jewish homeland in the Middle East.

The British, having been the only Allied power to fight in the region, believed they deserved control over most of the Middle East, including historical Mesopotamia, which became the new country of Iraq. The British sought to keep control of the Suez Canal, which linked the Mediterranean Sea and the Indian Ocean. They also wanted to maintain control over the newly discovered oil deposits in northern Iraq.

At the Versailles conference, Wilson proposed a vote that would allow the Arabs of the region to determine their own political future. However, the United Kingdom and France were both strongly opposed to independent nations

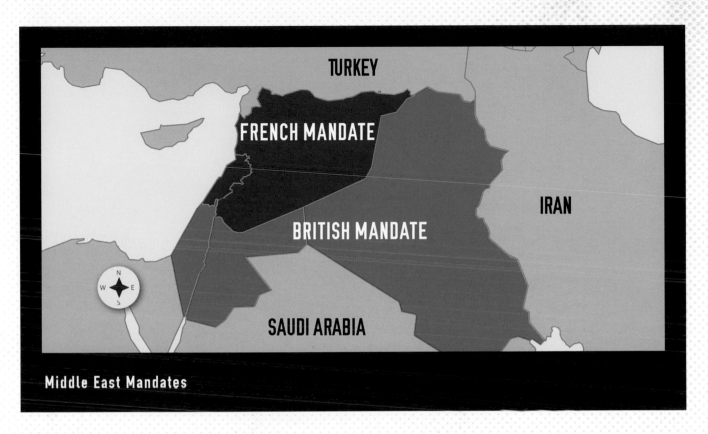

TURKEY

FRENCH MANDATE

BRITISH MANDATE

IRAN

SAUDI ARABIA

Middle East Mandates

in the Middle East. Ultimately, Wilson could not convince his allies to allow self-determination for the Arabs.

British and French diplomats set out the new boundaries of the Middle East. The result was a map that had little to do with the region's ethnic and cultural divisions. The new borders created turbulent and unstable states—and a cycle of violence that continues to this day.

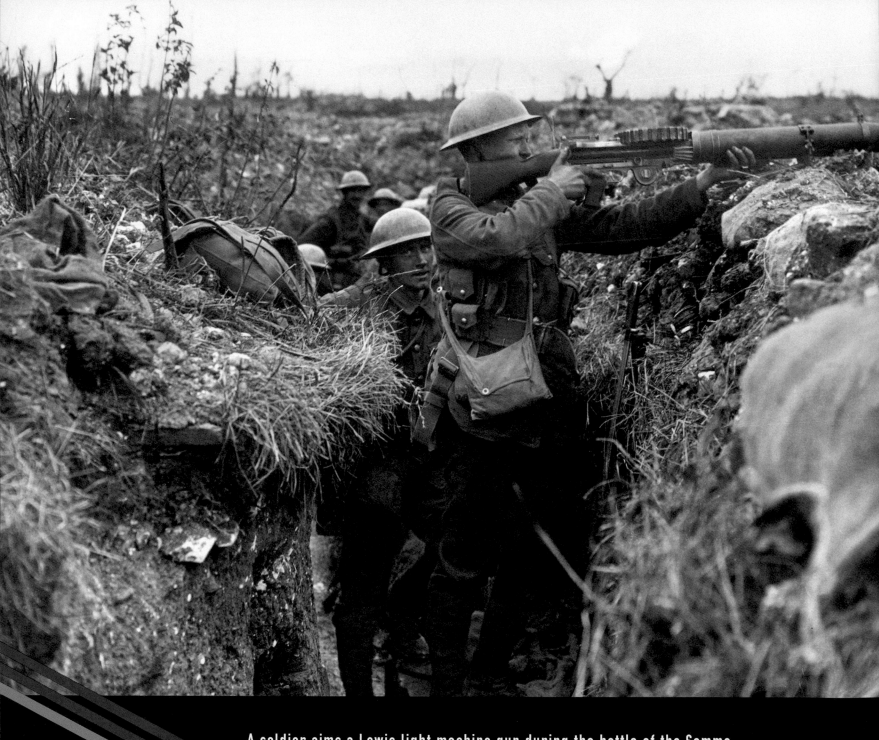

A soldier aims a Lewis light machine gun during the battle of the Somme.

HIGH-TECH WARFARE

The armies involved in World War I suffered high casualty rates. The grinding stalemate on the western front continued in a series of pointless assaults across the no-man's-land between the trenches. Soldiers marched across open ground against entrenched and brutally efficient machine guns. On the first day of the battle of the Somme, one of the bloodiest days of the war, the British suffered 19,000 deaths and 57,000 total casualties.[1]

Many generals schooled in the tactics of the 1800s did not understand the effect of new weapons and new technology on the battlefield. Massed infantry formations, for example, were vulnerable to artillery shelling as well as machine guns, which could spit large-caliber bullets across a battlefield at the rate of several hundred per minute. Many officers still favored obsolete infantry advances with bayonets fixed.

Generals on both sides stuck to the traditional unit formations, infantry assaults, and battle tactics in which they had been trained. The antiquated methods were futile against new technologies deployed on the battlefield: machine guns, hand and rifle grenades, flamethrowers, aerial bombing, and chemical weapons.

HEAVY STEEL

In the decades prior to World War I, advances in steelmaking and gun engineering created fearsome new artillery weapons. On the western front, the French deployed a 2.9-inch (75 mm) field artillery weapon that proved to be one of the most versatile and effective long-range guns in history.[2]

Traditional stone fortifications were no longer an effective defense for European cities. In the early days of the war, the German advance into Belgium paused before the cities of Liège and Namur. Although Belgian leaders believed these strongholds would protect their country, they soon discovered they had been planning for the previous war. The Germans' new Big Bertha, a 16.5-inch (420 mm) naval gun, was deployed on land.[3] Set in concrete to cushion its powerful recoil, the gun quickly reduced the massive stone fortifications of Liège and Namur to rubble.

German soldiers prepare to fire a Big Bertha gun.

Transport had always been a thorny problem for artillery and especially for high-caliber weapons that were too heavy for horse-and-wagon transport. For this reason, the Germans also developed the rail gun, which turned a railroad flatcar into a mobile gun platform. The gigantic Paris Gun was capable of hurling huge shells 70 miles (113 km).[4] The gun was inaccurate, but it had little trouble reaching the city limits of Paris and terrifying the populace. Instead of winning a tactical advantage on the battlefield, the Paris Gun was a propaganda weapon used to advertise German power and demoralize French civilians.

Transportation of heavy guns posed a major problem during World War I. After the war, new self-propelled guns were developed that did not require the use of trains or horses. These motorized guns, including the German 88 and the American 105-millimeter howitzer, depended on roads in good condition and well-trained crews who joined an entirely separate department of the regular army.

WEAPONS IN THE AIR

The development of military air forces during World War I transformed warfare over land and sea. Early in the war, airplanes were used mostly to watch enemy positions and movements. Airplanes could observe enemy trenches in preparation for a mass assault. Pilots dropped propaganda leaflets behind enemy lines and served as spotters for their own artillery batteries. Pilots used handguns for combat until 1915, when the Dutch aircraft engineer Anthony Fokker developed a synchronized machine gun that could fire forward between the blades of a spinning propeller.

A German attack on London during World War I was the first aerial bombardment of civilians in history. Giant, helium-filled airships known as

In addition to inventing an important weapon, Anthony Fokker was an excellent pilot.

Zeppelins regularly crossed the English Channel to raid British cities. The war also saw the first bombing of manufacturing facilities when the British attacked airship and submarine bases in Germany.

After the war, in the 1920s and 1930s, British war planners gave serious thought to the German bombing of civilian targets. Believing German bombers would have no trouble reaching the United Kingdom, the British built a coordinated civil defense network. Spotters along the coast watched for incoming aircraft, and a radio communications network allowed a coordinated defense. The development of fast, maneuverable fighter planes, including the Hurricane and Spitfire, helped the United Kingdom survive a massive assault by the German air force in 1940.

The use of airplanes as military weapons during World War I brought about the invention of the aircraft carrier. These huge ships allowed navies to attack enemies at much greater distances. In World War II, strategic bombing of cities and industries proved a decisive weapon.

A NEW SHIP

The first ship designed to allow takeoff and landing of airplanes was the HMS *Argus*, a British vessel. Converted from a passenger liner, the *Argus* had a flight deck 549 feet (167 m) long.[6] Although the ship was commissioned too late to serve in World War I, navies around the world were quick to develop new carrier designs after the war.

Aircraft carriers have become the backbone of the modern US Navy and other maritime forces around the world.

CHEMICAL WEAPONS

World War I also saw the first use of one of the most frightening weapons ever invented, the poison gas shell. The Germans began using chemical weapons in April 1915, near the Belgian city of Ypres. Chlorine gas seeped out of 6,000 canisters and floated toward the Allied trenches.[5] Men who came in contact with the poisonous cloud convulsed as the gas filled and paralyzed their lungs. A British soldier described the attack:

> Figures [were] running wildly in confusion over the fields. Greenish-gray clouds swept down upon them, turning yellow as they traveled over the country blasting everything they touched and shriveling up the vegetation. . . . Then there staggered into our midst French soldiers, blinded, coughing, chests heaving, faces an ugly purple color, lips speechless with agony, and behind them in the gas soaked trenches, we learned that they had left hundreds of dead and dying comrades.[7]

Chemical weapons terrified and demoralized enemy soldiers. When the gas drifted away from battlefields and through nearby villages, it also reached civilians. But gas was difficult to control and proved in many cases to be just as dangerous to the men who deployed it. Approximately 90,000 deaths were attributed to chemical weapons during World War I.[8]

CIVILIANS IN WARTIME

Prior to World War I, wars were largely fought away from population centers. But in 1914, the German army left behind the traditional view that civilians should remain outside of the conflict on the battlefield. As the German army swept into Belgium, the occasional hidden sniper taking aim at German infantry sparked massive reprisals against local civilians. In several towns, men, women, and children were rounded up and executed by German troops. The attack on civilians prompted angry editorials in newspapers in the United Kingdom and the United States, increasing civilian support for the war in those countries.

These weapons were used despite the Hague Convention of 1907 and the Hague Declaration of 1899, both of which forbid the use of poison gas in wartime.

Germany's chemical industry was the world's most advanced. German commanders believed their secret weapon would provide the means to a swift victory on the stalemated western front. At Ypres, they were not quite prepared for the effectiveness of gas. Their own troops greatly feared the yellowish clouds and were unable to take advantage of the break in the Allied line they created.

The British quickly developed gas masks to counter the array of chemical weapons, which included chlorine, mustard gas, phosgene gas, and tear gas. The masks were uncomfortable and made it difficult to see, but they prevented extensive casualties. Even horses were fitted with gas masks. In the United States, a new military agency known as the Chemical Warfare Service, part of the US Army, was created to develop both offensive chemical weapons and defensive countermeasures. The Geneva Protocol of 1925 banned the use of

A DANGEROUS LEGACY

The use of chemical weapons terrified soldiers on World War I battlefields and caused an estimated 88,500 deaths.[9] In 1925, the Geneva Protocol banned the use of chemical weapons during wartime. The treaty did not prohibit the manufacture or stockpiling of these weapons, however, which continued all over the world, including in the United States. In the 1980s, Iraq violated the Geneva Protocol by deploying chemical weapons against Iran. A new Chemical Weapons Convention, which went into force in 1997, sets as its goal the destruction of all chemical weapons in existence.

Gas masks helped protect soldiers and horses from chemical weapons.

chemical weapons by nations that signed the treaty. Although both Germany and the United States held to this agreement during World War II, other nations, including Italy during its invasion of Ethiopia in 1935, did not.

SUBMARINES

Invented decades prior to World War I, the underwater vessel came into its own as a military weapon during World War I. Sonar—echoing sound waves that detect underwater objects such as submarines—had not been invented. The German submarines, known as U-boats, were silent and invisible from the surface. The German U-boat fleet attacked merchant shipping between North America and Europe with deadly effectiveness.

Although they were relatively slow, submarines could maneuver freely through coastal waters and along busy shipping lanes. A single torpedo could cripple a large vessel or send valuable cargo to the bottom of the sea. Submarines could also attack military targets, although both sides developed effective antisubmarine weapons during the war.

TANKS

The first tanks, also known as landships, rolled off British assembly lines during World War I. These were armor-plated cars with continuous tracks for climbing over rough terrain. On clear and level ground, the landship could reach a top speed of three miles per hour (5 kmh).[10]

The British first deployed tanks on September 15, 1916, during a battle at Delville Wood, in France. The French followed with their first tank assault in April 1917 during the Aisne Offensive. The machines suffered frequent breakdowns, but they posed a tough challenge for the Germans, who had no means, other than heavy artillery, to stop or slow them. In November 1917, the British massed 474 tanks at the battle of Cambrai, creating a huge breach in the German lines and leading to the capture of 10,000 German prisoners.[11]

A British tank makes its way over a German trench.

The German army brought its own tanks to the battlefield in April 1918, but Germany managed to produce only 20 of the machines during the war.[12] For the Allies, tanks provided a crucial battlefield advantage when used in coordination with aircraft and artillery to clear a path for infantry. The tank, rather than massed artillery or machine guns, made the war of the trenches obsolete. Tanks could easily plow through barbed wire and cross enemy trenches, punching holes in the line for infantry to exploit. They made warfare more mobile and allowed armies to move faster and farther once an enemy's lines were breached. The tank made possible the blitzkrieg, or "lightning war," the German army unleashed in Europe and North Africa during World War II.

World War I destroyed much of Europe's transportation infrastructure, including bridges.

ECONOMIC BUSTS AND BOOMS

The massive casualties and physical destruction wrought by World War I were paralleled by serious economic damage. The war dealt national economies on both sides a severe blow, in ways that were hard for the combatants to foresee at the start of the war.

For the British and the French, the war effort depended on borrowed money. After the armistice, repayments seriously burdened the Allied governments, which could not make needed investments in their railroads and port facilities. The financial situation was even worse in Germany, a country that owed billions in war reparations as mandated by the Treaty of Versailles.

The war damaged transport systems in Europe, making it more difficult for exporters to get their goods to market. Throughout the continent, demand for goods fell, factories shut down, and millions of able-bodied workers were thrown out of work. This put added pressure on governments to fund public benefits to support the long-term unemployed, as well as disabled veterans.

The new borders drawn after the war also disrupted trade on the continent. For example, Austria no longer had access to coal; this resource came from mines in Poland, which was now an independent country. As a result, the cities of Austria and other nations in Central Europe suffered shortages of electricity and fuel for heating.

The destruction of productive farmland, shortages of seed and fertilizers, and the breaks in the rail network through war damage contributed to famine and disease epidemics. New sicknesses appeared, including Spanish influenza, which was first recorded in January 1918. By the time the Spanish influenza subsided in 1919, it had killed more soldiers and civilians than did actual fighting. The illness had a high mortality rate and spread rapidly through the movement of merchant ships and military transports around the globe. In the United States alone, Spanish flu affected one-quarter of the population, and the average life expectancy dropped by approximately ten years as a result.[1]

Medical workers wore masks to protect themselves from the Spanish influenza.

ECONOMIC EFFECTS IN THE UNITED STATES

While Europe faced a postwar crisis, the United States had escaped the war with its economy—as well as its factories, farms, and railroads—intact. President Wilson sought to provide food relief to Europe but found European leaders fearful of American businessmen seizing control of their markets.

In 1921, the American government did step in with the American Relief Administration. The federal government contributed $100 million, and American farmers used the relief program to dispose of large surpluses of grain.[2] The US Food Administration built distribution centers and soup kitchens. The organization also provided transport for food, medical supplies, and clothing.

The war had boosted industrial production in the United States. The country experienced 44 months of economic growth between 1914 and 1918.[3] By waiting three years to join the war effort, the United States had allowed its manufacturing sector to gradually adapt to wartime needs by selling to eager European customers. By 1917, American factories were well prepared to meet the war's demands when the US military finally set sail for France.

After the armistice, the United States went through an economic recession. Inflation rose, making goods more expensive. The dollar rose in value against European currencies, making American products more expensive and tougher for companies to sell in foreign nations. Returning soldiers flooded the labor market, increasing the competition for scarce jobs.

By 1920, however, the economy was growing. Factories using new technologies such as the automated assembly line met rising demand for consumer goods including radios and automobiles. A wave of homebuilding swept the cities as rural families moved to urban areas for better jobs and living conditions. For the first time, merchants accepted installment payments, or buying on credit.

BARRIERS TO TRADE

After World War I, many countries were desperate to protect their own industries from foreign competition. As a result, they began charging higher tariffs—taxes due on imported goods. These tariffs made foreign products more expensive for

A FEAR OF IMMIGRANTS

A desire to stay free of European troubles inspired the US Congress to pass new immigration restrictions in 1917. New arrivals had to pass a literacy test and pay a tax. After the war, despite a prospering economy and general peace around the globe, many American politicians still saw immigrants as a threat to the general health and welfare of the country.

In 1921, Congress passed the first immigrant quota law. Each year, immigration from each country would be limited to 3 percent of the number of people from that country who were already in the United States as of 1910.[4] The system of quotas as a means to restrict legal immigration has survived to the present day.

consumers. However, this action also prompted the targeted countries to raise their own tariffs in retaliation. The rising costs of imports slowed international trade, which, according to one economic historian, took 80 years to recover.[5]

The war restricted people as well as goods. Passports were not common before the war, so there had been few barriers to immigration. Worried over national security, the US Congress passed new restrictions on immigration. The war also changed governments' positions on finance. For example, the massive borrowing needed to pay for the war effort prompted the British government to spend heavily while the economy was shrinking. As a result, taxes rose along with the public debt. Currencies, once fixed to the value of gold, were allowed to fluctuate freely in relative value.

Many governments, including that of the United States, saw they had an important role to play in the economy and providing a social safety net; this included benefits for the unemployed, the elderly, and veterans. This approach led to the creation of a new federal agency in the United States, the National Recovery Administration (NRA). When an economic crisis hit the United States and the rest of the world in the early 1930s, the government responded with New Deal programs. The New Deal was a response to mass unemployment, widespread bank failures, and the collapse of lending. The NRA provided jobs and set wage standards for businesses.

The Civilian Conservation Corps (CCC) was one of the many New Deal programs. These CCC workers cleared dead trees at Arlington National Cemetery.

CRISIS IN GERMANY

The German government was the last of the Central powers to seek peace terms with the Allies. The war had deprived Germany of land as well as productive industrial regions in the east and west. German industries lost a huge number of workers: the German war dead numbered 1.8 million.[6] Germany also struggled with a lack of credit, as businesses found it more difficult and expensive to borrow money. The massive reparations imposed by the Treaty of Versailles drained the public treasury and crippled the government's ability to provide relief or economic stimulus. The German economy all but collapsed, unemployment increased, and prices steadily rose.

Germany, similar to the United Kingdom, had financed its war effort by borrowing money. After the war's end, the German government had difficulty raising money by selling bonds, as many other countries refused to deal with the defeated nation. There seemed to be only one way to raise money and pay workers: by simply printing more money. However, as more currency flowed into the system, the value of money fell, and prices skyrocketed.

By 1923, hyperinflation was turning German currency, the reichsmark, into worthless scrap paper. Workers collected their wages in the form of huge bricks of currency, which were transported in wheelbarrows and spent immediately before prices could rise again. In November, it took one trillion reichsmarks to buy a single US dollar.[7] Savings accounts were wiped out, and most people had to barter for their household goods. The crisis came to a head in late 1923, when the exchange rate reached 4.2 trillion reichsmarks to the US dollar.[8]

Under the direction of banker Hjalmar Schacht, Germany eased the crisis by creating a new currency, the rentenmark. Mortgages and factory loans backed the new currency, and reichsmarks were dropped from circulation. One rentenmark equaled one billion reichsmarks.[9]

Instability, hyperinflation, and a loss of faith in the new German government set the stage for a charismatic leader who promised to restore Germany's place as the economic and military superpower of Europe. Adolf Hitler and his Nazi Party gained support through the 1920s, winning seats in the German legislature and pushing for Germany to denounce the Versailles treaty.

GERMAN CURRENCY RECOVERS

In an attempt to keep vital industrial workers paid and on the job, the German government made a disastrous financial mistake: printing the money needed to meet payrolls. By the fall of 1923, German currency was all but worthless.

Although the old reichsmarks went out of circulation in November of that year, their value has since revived around the world. Many collectors now specialize in German "inflation currency" originally printed in 1923.

To speed up the printing process, these notes were printed on only one side. They carried limited dates of validity, from a few weeks up to three months. Some were issued by private companies, such as the Stinnes Shipping Lines of Hamburg. In 2015, a currency dealer offered a set of three Stinnes notes with face values of 1 million, 5 million, and 10 million reichsmarks. When they were issued, the notes were worth less than a penny; in 2015, they sold for $19.50.[10]

The radical deflation that followed the collapse of Germany's currency threw the nation into a cycle of business failures and rising unemployment. Prices and wages actually fell, while investment and lending came to a standstill; investors had no faith in the future and no expectation of a gain for lending money or buying shares. The result was a banking crisis in Germany and Austria in 1931 that boosted the appeal of radical political parties, including Adolf Hitler's.

The memory of this economic catastrophe affects Germany to this day, with its people wary of lending money to nations, such as Greece, with weaker economies. Germans fear inflation

A German woman used reichsmarks to light her stove because the currency was worth so little.

above all and strongly favor balanced government budgets and conservative economic policies.

By the early 2000s, Germany, France, and other nations—rich and poor—had joined the European Union (EU). The EU sets strict fiscal policies for its members, including a limit on budget deficits and a ban on bailouts. A bailout is a situation in which a country facing bankruptcy is given financial support. In large part, these policies stem from the economic aftermath of World War I.

THE DAWES PLAN SAVES GERMANY

The heavy burden of Germany's reparations payments proved too much for the German government, which managed only a single full payment in 1921. After hyperinflation destroyed the German currency in 1923, the United States stepped in with the Dawes Plan. Named after Vice President Charles Dawes, the plan set lower targets for the reparations payments and loaned money to stabilize the German economy and currency. For five years, Germany enjoyed economic growth. It lasted until 1929, which marked the beginning of the Great Depression, a period of worldwide economic downturn.

Czech troops marched beside their president's car in the new nation of Czechoslovakia.

CHANGES IN THE GLOBAL MAP

World War I resulted in drastic changes in the map of Europe. New countries were created, while old empires vanished. International boundaries drawn by the Versailles Conference raised new barriers to the movement of people and goods across the continent. This affected trade, investment, and national economies. The new borders and new countries also gave rise to resentments and grievances that would fester for generations and in some cases are still very much alive.

THE END OF AUSTRIA-HUNGARY

Home to 11 nationalities, 14 languages, and more than 50 million people, Austria-Hungary had done more than any other nation to set off World War I.[1] By October 1918, however, the empire was pressing for peace. After the death of Emperor Franz Joseph in 1916, his son and successor, Charles, was prepared to reach an agreement with the Allies to end the war.

Woodrow Wilson's Fourteen Points had set out the principle of self-determination. By this principle, it would be up to the Czechs, Hungarians,

THE LAST EMPEROR

Charles, the last ruler of the Hapsburg Empire, gave up his throne as the government of Austria-Hungary collapsed in the fall of 1918. Charles was exiled to Madeira, a remote island in the Atlantic Ocean, where he died of pneumonia in 1922.

The last Hapsburg emperor was not forgotten, however. A devout Catholic, he earned praise from church leaders for his voluntary and peaceful abdication. In the view of many, Charles sacrificed his own interests for those of the people living in the Hapsburg dominions. After World War II, the church began a campaign to declare him a saint. In 2004, Pope John Paul II declared the beatification of Charles—the last step before sainthood. To reach that goal, however, the church requires a verified miracle.

Charles may be rewarded. In 2008, a woman from Kissimmee, Florida, claimed she was cured of cancer by praying to Charles. She immediately converted from the Baptist church to Catholicism. To investigate, the church convened a council, which found no scientific explanation for the woman's dramatic recovery. As of 2015, the case was still pending at the Vatican, the headquarters of the Catholic Church.

Slovaks, Croats, and other nationalities ruled by the Hapsburgs to declare their intentions.

At this time, the Czechs living in the northern reaches of the empire and the Slavs living in the south were organizing independent governments in readiness for the imminent peace. The Hungarians set up a National Committee on October 24, while Polish leaders also set up a committee and were demanding northern provinces of the old empire, including Silesia and Galicia.

On October 30, representatives of German-speaking regions within Austria-Hungary proclaimed their own separate, ethnic German nation, to be carved out of the northeastern provinces lying south and west of Vienna, the imperial capital. On November 3, Italy and Austria-Hungary signed a formal armistice. The Austro-Hungarian army was to withdraw from all territory it had occupied since the start of the war, as well as the province of Istria, which bordered the Adriatic Sea.

REWARDS FOR SERVICE

Although three empires had fallen as a result of World War I, the British Empire survived. In addition to its new mandates in the Middle East, the United Kingdom still held India, Burma, and South Africa. For their assistance during the war, Britain rewarded some of its territories with new mandates of their own. Australia, for example, was given German New Guinea, which is now Papua New Guinea; South Africa received the former German colony of Southwest Africa, which is modern Namibia; and New Zealand won German Samoa, now part of independent Samoa.

On November 11, Emperor Charles formally gave up his right to take part in the Austrian government's affairs. The Hapsburg dynasty, after ruling one of the most powerful European states for seven centuries, came to an abrupt end.

The dismemberment of the Austro-Hungarian Empire took place through a series of treaties. The Treaty of Trianon in 1920 recognized the independent state of Hungary, while the Treaty of Saint-Germain established the new, German-speaking republic of Austria. Lands once belonging to the kingdom of Hungary were made part of Romania, Czechoslovakia, and the newly created Kingdom of the Serbs, Croats, and Slovenes. The creation of ethnic minorities in Hungary, Romania, and

Emperor Charles I was the last ruler of the Hapsburg Empire.

Czechoslovakia led to social and political tensions in Central Europe, which were exploited by new political parties in the 1930s.

The redrawn borders had the effect of making Hungary a landlocked, isolated country without direct access to sea transportation. Rising unemployment in the country led to social turbulence through the next decade. Hungary's resentment over the terms of the Treaty of Trianon threw the nation into an alliance with Hitler and the Nazis during the 1930s.

The Slavs had a historic grievance against the Austria-Hungary Compromise of 1867, which had cut them out of power at the top. Now, with World War I over and Austria-Hungary consigned to history, Slavic leaders were worried about Italy's desire to seize the eastern coast of the Adriatic Sea and also the possibility of war breaking out between Serbia and Croatia. On December 1, 1918, the Kingdom of the Serbs, Croats, and Slovenes was formed, with the Serbian Karadjordjevic dynasty at its head. This state lasted until 1929, when the republic of Yugoslavia was proclaimed.

The melting pot of the South Slavs remained intact after World War II, when a centralized communist regime was established under strongman Josip Broz Tito. The nation remained intact until the 1990s when, after Tito's death, it was pulled apart in a civil war and divided into six separate countries.

Some historians draw parallels between Austria-Hungary and the modern European Union. Similar to the EU, Austria-Hungary was a union of many

Yugoslavian President Josip Broz Tito speaks before the country's national assembly.

different nationalities. And also like the EU, Austria-Hungary could never seem to resolve demands from smaller, poorer groups within its borders for self-determination and economic independence.

THE REBIRTH OF POLAND

In the late 1500s, the kings of Poland ruled one of the largest empires in Europe. By the end of the 1700s, the country had vanished from the map. Russia,

Austria-Hungary, and Prussia had partitioned the kingdom and seized Polish territory adjoining their borders.

The Versailles treaty gave birth to a new Polish republic. This time, the seizure of land worked in the opposite direction. Poland was granted lands that had belonged to Germany and Austria-Hungary prior to 1914. Poland also gained a strip of territory that gave the country access to the Baltic Sea. Known as the Danzig Corridor, this area had a large population of ethnic Germans. East Prussia, the easternmost province of the old German Empire, remained under Germany's control but became an island territory, cut off from the rest of Germany.

Germany's loss of this vast swath of land gave German nationalists a serious grievance against the Allies and the Treaty of Versailles. Once a prosperous nation with a growing population, Germany now was a cramped, poor, defeated shell of its former self. The growth of the Nazi Party through the 1920s largely resulted from the anger among ordinary Germans at this perceived injustice. Hitler came to power promising revenge for the stab in the back that had defeated Germany. Hitler also sought lebensraum, or "living space," for displaced ethnic Germans in the east.

BRITISH COLONIES
WESTERN RULERS OPPOSE EASTERN INDEPENDENCE

Victory in World War I did not encourage the British government to liberate its many overseas colonies. Even though Indians had fought in the trenches on the western front, a movement for self-rule, led by the young lawyer Mohandas Gandhi, faced stern opposition among British leaders, including Winston Churchill.

Gandhi had encouraged Indians to fight for the Allies during World War I, believing this support for the British war effort would lead the grateful colonial master to grant them self-rule. Although 1.5 million Indians volunteered for service in combat and noncombat roles, Gandhi was mistaken. The British government would not even allow India the same semi-independent status enjoyed by the territories of Australia, South Africa, and Canada. British Foreign Secretary Arthur Balfour explained why:

> *East is East and West is West. Even in the West, parliamentary institutions have rarely been a success, except among English-speaking peoples. In the East, not only have they never been seriously tried, but they have never been desired, except by intellectuals who have come under Western influences.*[2]

The British colonies of Mesopotamia, Burma, and East Africa did not receive self-rule either. Instead, the principle of self-determination—proclaimed as an important goal of the Versailles conference—applied only to nations in Europe. Indeed, the United Kingdom's overseas colonial empire reached its greatest extent after the signing of the Versailles treaty.

Where the British government did grant independence, as in Egypt, it came with conditions. Although the people of Egypt were permitted a sovereign government, the British kept control of the Suez Canal, which ran between Egypt and the Sinai Peninsula, linking the Mediterranean Sea with the Indian Ocean.

Gandhi, a firm believer in pacifism and nonviolent resistance, was a leader of the Indian independence movement.

Most people read about the war in newspapers and did not directly experience the conflict.

CHAPTER

6

THE LEAGUE OF NATIONS

The major battles of World War I took place in northern France, Belgium, the Balkan Mountains, western Russia, and the mountainous borderlands between Italy and Austria. Most of the continent was far from the battle zones, and most civilians did not have firsthand experience of the war's horrors.

But the media brought home the war. Newspapers carried daily first-page dispatches from the front and reprinted letters from soldiers who revealed the war's hardships, dangers, and fears. The long casualty lists were a daily reminder that war, even one fought from a sense of national honor, carried a very heavy price.

By late 1918, the casualty lists had stretched to the millions. A war that was widely expected to be over quickly, fought over a political squabble in Central Europe, had turned into a catastrophe. In an article published in a London paper, the British author H. G. Wells used the phrase "the war that will end war."[1] There was a consensus that Europe had to find a different way to settle its age-old disputes. If they could only meet and talk things out, debate their disputes, and air their grievances, perhaps the nations of the world could avoid another episode of mass killing and destruction.

A GUIDING HAND

The European powers had met in a series of congresses during the 1800s. Diplomats held these high-level summits to resolve disputes and redraw borders after the close of a war. In 1815, the Congress of Vienna had settled things after the fall of French emperor Napoleon. After a conflict between Russia and the Ottoman Empire, the Congress of Berlin redrew borders in the Balkans in 1878. But these meetings never seemed to permanently resolve disputes. The treaties and alliances designed to achieve a lasting peace had instead entangled the European nations in the Great War that had just ended.

At the end of World War I, the United States made an attempt to decide the future of Europe. For most of the war, the Americans had stayed neutral. When they finally joined the Allies in 1917, their army played a decisive role in the

Vittorio Emanuele Orlando of Italy, David Lloyd George of the United Kingdom, Georges Clemenceau of France, and Woodrow Wilson of the United States met after the war ended.

defeat of Germany. President Wilson enjoyed great prestige in Europe and was greeted as a conquering hero in London and Paris. Wilson's Fourteen Points had formed the basis of the November 1918 armistice that had stopped the fighting on the western front. The United States still deployed an army that could step in where needed and persuade any nation reluctant to agree to the president's terms.

As a result, Wilson was in a very good position to make suggestions, including the idea of a permanent international diplomatic organization. The goal would be to get negotiations and treaties out into the open; there would be no more secret deals. The very first of the Fourteen Points called for "Open covenants of peace, openly arrived at."[2] Many believed secret agreements among the European leaders were one of the primary causes of the war.

The future organization, which came to be known as the League of Nations, might also serve as a way for people held under colonial or foreign rule to achieve self-determination. This principle was behind the breakup of Austria-Hungary, the new Kingdom of the Serbs, the rebirth of Poland, and the creation of Czechoslovakia. Newly independent states, free to form their own governments as they saw fit, would be less likely to turn to larger empires to fight their battles, as the Serbs had turned to the Russians. Instead, all countries could bring their grievances to the league, which would give a voice to every sovereign nation, no matter how new, small, or poor that nation might be.

IDEALISM THAT WASN'T IDEAL

As part of the Fourteen Points, Wilson had proclaimed the right of all peoples to national self-determination. Although European leaders proclaimed their general support of this idea, outside their own continent they would be slow to put it into practice.

Rather than giving European colonies their independence, the Versailles treaty simply shifted their ownership. The goal was not national self-determination but the punishment of the war's losers. The territory of German East Africa, for example, was handed to the United Kingdom, Portugal, and Belgium. These lands did not achieve independence until after World War II. They include the modern nations of Burundi, Mozambique, Rwanda, and Tanzania.

THE COVENANT OF THE LEAGUE

At Versailles, however, negotiations were not always peaceful. The battles on the western front turned into a war of words among the United Kingdom, France, Italy, and the United States. The European powers were not enthusiastic about the creation of a League of Nations. Instead, they were more interested in gaining what they felt they deserved for winning the war. They also wanted to hold on to their valuable colonies without the interference of President Wilson or the United States.

Wilson was persuasive, however. To get matters settled, the United Kingdom and France went along with the league, and Wilson turned a blind eye to their colonial rule in the Middle East, Africa, and Asia. The Covenant of the League of Nations was created with the Versailles treaty in 1919. By December 1920, 48 nations had signed the covenant and joined the organization.

OPPOSITION IN CONGRESS

The league worked as intended in the 1920s. Debates at league conferences allowed Germany to settle a dispute with Poland over the region of Upper Silesia. Italy solved a problem it had with Greece, and Greece settled matters with Bulgaria.

One member not present in these debates or any other was the United States. On returning home after his triumph at Versailles, Wilson faced strong opposition to the league in Congress. Many of these elected representatives did not want to commit the United States to the league and possibly place American interests at the mercy of an international organization. In addition, lawmakers did not want the United States dragged into another European war—and many believed the league was likely to do just that.

In an attempt to get American voters behind the league, Wilson made speeches, wrote articles, took a presidential train on tour, and pushed himself to a state of total exhaustion. But he could do little to sway the opposed representatives, particularly Henry Cabot Lodge, the Senate majority leader. During one speech against the Versailles treaty and the league, Lodge commented:

> You may call me selfish if you will, conservative or reactionary, or use any other harsh adjective you see fit to apply, but an American I was born, an American I have remained all my life. I can never be anything else but an American, and I must think of the United States first, and when I think of the United States first in an arrangement like this I am thinking of what is best for the world, for if the United States fails, the best hopes of mankind fail with it. I have had but one allegiance—I cannot divide it now.[3]

The US Congress voted against the league in 1920, and Wilson's successors had no interest in reviving the idea or proposing any changes to it. The League

The first meeting of the League of Nations took place in Geneva, Switzerland, on November 15, 1920.

Senate majority leader Henry Cabot Lodge opposed the League of Nations.

of Nations came into being, but without the participation of the United States. As a result, the league was led by countries that were militarily and economically powerful—the same countries that had brought about World War I.

THE LEAGUE FADES AWAY

In the 1930s, the league met aggression with a weak response. Japan ignored league sanctions while it invaded Manchuria, a region of China on the Asian mainland. After Italy invaded Ethiopia in 1935, economic sanctions agreed to by league members achieved nothing. The league also failed to impose an oil embargo that would have stopped the Italian army in its tracks. The league tried, and failed, to put into effect a Convention on Terrorism. This convention would have required nations that signed the document to pass laws allowing other countries to request the transfer of suspected terrorists.

When Germany took control of Austria in 1938 and later seized Czechoslovakia, the league could offer no response. The league had no army, and the United Kingdom and France were unwilling to go to war over the matter even though the Czechoslovakia, as a member of the league, was supposed to enjoy its protection.

The league did nothing to stop Germany's invasion of Poland in 1939, an event that touched off World War II. This war took place on an even larger scale than World War I, even though Germany had supposedly been rendered militarily powerless by the Treaty of Versailles.

The idea of an international organization to resolve disputes survived, however. In June 1945, representatives of 50 countries met in San Francisco, California, to sign a United Nations Charter.[4] The new organization matched its purpose to that of the League of Nations: to provide a forum to resolve international disputes. The charter included a Security Council, to be made up of four superpowers that would have the authority to veto any act or resolution of the entire organization. This time, the new organization, known as the United Nations, started with the full participation of the United States.

THE END OF THE LEAGUE

The League of Nations was designed to draw nations together to avoid another world war. But the league could do nothing to check the aggression of Germany, Italy, and Japan in the 1930s. The final blow to the league's prestige was a spat between the Soviet Union and the United States. When President Franklin Roosevelt publicly criticized the Soviet invasion of Finland in 1939, the Soviets retaliated by announcing they would not participate in the New York World's Fair, to be held in 1940. As one of its last actions, the League of Nations expelled the Soviet Union from its ranks.

The Germany army began its invasion of Poland in September 1939.

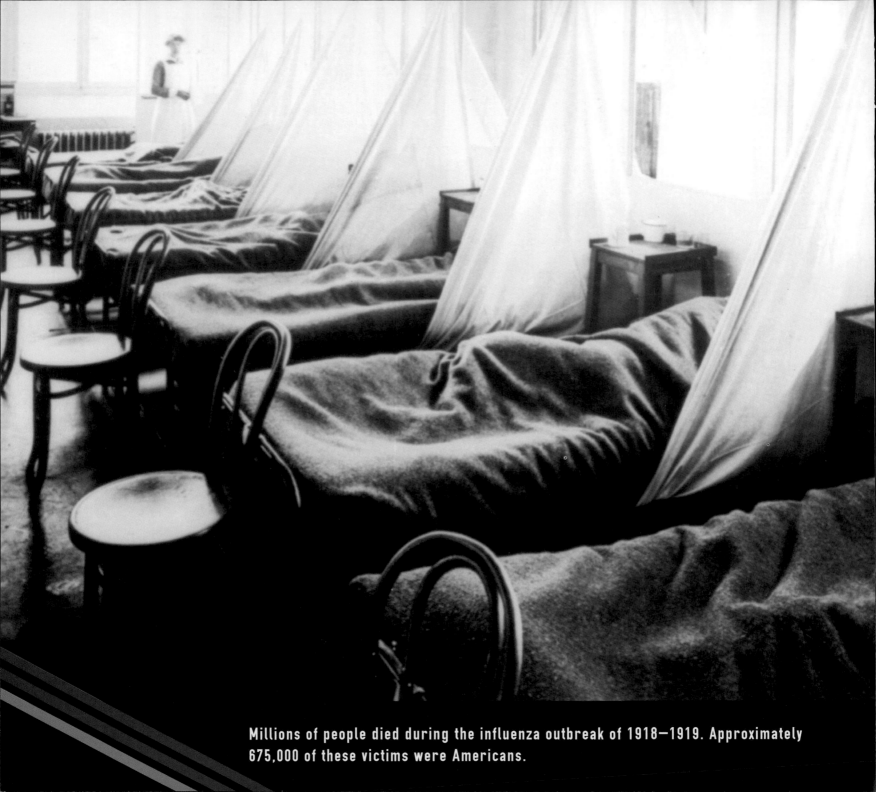

Millions of people died during the influenza outbreak of 1918—1919. Approximately 675,000 of these victims were Americans.

★ 7 ★

TURMOIL IN THE UNITED STATES

The United States escaped the war with far fewer deaths than France, the United Kingdom, or Germany. Nevertheless, war deaths as a percentage of troops in the conflict was high for the United States. In addition, the influenza outbreak of 1918–1919 was spread in large part by the military transports that traveled the seas between Europe and North America.

In Europe, President Wilson was a hero for throwing the economic and military power of the United States behind the Allies. In many ways, Wilson and the United States seemed above the terrible fray. Americans showed no ambition to seize new territory or punish the losing side. As Wilson often proclaimed, the

THE INFLUENZA SEASON

In areas where battles took place, World War I degraded medical facilities, making it easier for disease epidemics to spread. Although civilians in the United States lived far from the battlefields of Europe, disease still had an effect at home when an influenza outbreak spread worldwide in 1918.

Victims died in days or even hours, their lungs filling with fluid and their respiratory systems shutting down completely. By some estimates, more than 50 million people died of influenza during and shortly after the war—a death toll three times that of the war itself.[1]

The influenza had a significant effect on society. With so many people ill, schools and businesses closed. Garbage went uncollected, and mail went undelivered. Thousands of children became orphans. The outbreak finally subsided in the summer of 1919.

US government simply wanted the peace terms to settle Europe's disputes, establish democracy among nations that wanted it, and prevent another world war.

At home, however, things were not always so peaceful. During the war, the scarcity of labor drove up wages for factory workers. Workers and employers agreed to keep the peace with a "no strike" policy, while manufacturers were guaranteed a minimum profit on goods produced for the government. When the war ended, returning veterans flooded the labor market, but employers were not hiring—instead, they were laying off workers and closing down factories. Inflation surged in the United States, driving up prices and eating away at savings. Demand for goods was low in war-torn Europe, and protective tariffs raised by countries trying to bring their economies back to health were making it difficult to export at a profit.

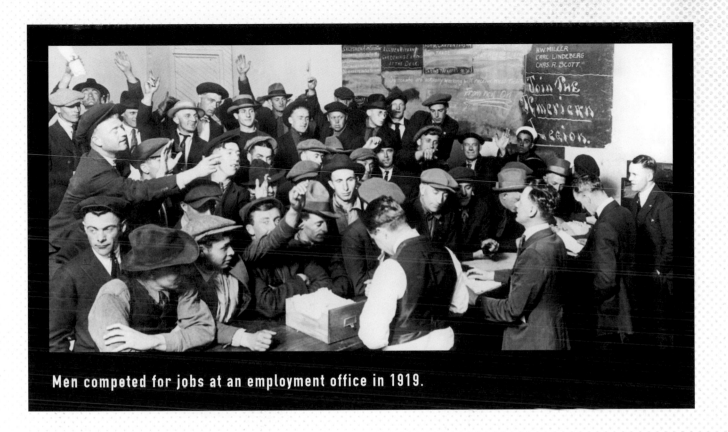

Men competed for jobs at an employment office in 1919.

WALKING OFF THE JOB

Labor trouble began soon after the war's end. The Industrial Workers of the World (IWW), began organizing workers on a mass scale. The IWW unions grew powerful in steel and other essential industries. In early 1919, a labor war erupted in Seattle, Washington, where a general strike in February shut down factories and shops and paralyzed the city. The mayor of Seattle, Ole Hanson, called out the militia and threatened mass arrests while warning the populace of an imminent communist takeover of the city by workers and union bosses.

Hanson's words found a receptive audience. Many people saw the Russian Revolution of October 1917 as only the beginning. Bolsheviks were opposed to democracy and free-market capitalism and were threatening revolutions in Germany, France, and Italy. The end of the war provided socialist parties an opportunity to recruit soldiers and civilians who saw the war's four years of slaughter as a failure of the political and economic systems already in place.

In September 1919, a potentially more dangerous strike took place among the Boston police, who were protesting low wages, long hours, and wretched conditions at the station houses where they lived. Seeking to form a union and join the American Federation of Labor (AFL), the police walked off the job when their demands were unmet. Looting and general mayhem broke out the same evening in many Boston neighborhoods.

The resulting panic among the citizenry prompted Governor Calvin Coolidge to call out the state militia to patrol the streets and restore order. Asserting that police should not have the right to form unions and that the strike posed a grave danger to the public, Coolidge sent a stern telegram to AFL president Samuel Gompers, which stated, "There is no right to strike against the public safety by anyone, anytime, anywhere."[2]

His terse words won national attention. The Republican Party nominated Coolidge for the vice presidency at the side of candidate Warren G. Harding in

1920. Harding won the election in November of that year, and upon his death in 1923, Coolidge attained the White House.

THE RED SCARE

Politicians in the United States were quick to play on the fears of what they termed the Red Menace. As evidence, they pointed to worsening labor strife, the socialist revolutions in Europe, and the violent acts of anarchists throughout the world. Leading the charge was Attorney General A. Mitchell Palmer.

In August 1919, a powerful bomb exploded on Palmer's front porch in Washington, DC, killing the individual who was carrying it. Other bombs were

SUCCESSFUL SUFFRAGETTES

The demand among women for suffrage—the right to vote—had simmered for decades. But the governments of the United States and most other nations held voting as a traditional right of adult male citizens. Many people believed women did not have the proper interest or knowledge of public affairs to vote responsibly. In the opinion of many leaders, women should stay out of the grubby fields of politics and elections altogether.

World War I played an important part in changing this outlook. Women played a major role in war industries, served at the front as nurses, and led several international drives for a truce to stop the fighting. At its end, the war appeared to many as a monumental political and diplomatic blunder that had been committed exclusively by men. Over the following decade, several countries, including the United States with the Nineteenth Amendment to the Constitution, gave women the right to vote in national elections.

mailed to business leaders, and the public grew worried over the prospects of an impending violent revolution—a Bolshevik uprising in America.

In an article entitled "The Case Against the Reds," published in 1920, Palmer laid out his case for the drastic action the Department of Justice undertook in 1919:

> *Like a prairie-fire, the blaze of revolution was sweeping over every American institution of law and order a year ago. It was eating its way into the homes of the American workman, its sharp tongues of revolutionary heat were licking the alters of the churches, leaping into the belfry of the school bell, crawling into the sacred corners of American homes, seeking to replace marriage vows with libertine laws, burning up the foundations of society.[3]*

Palmer organized the General Intelligence Unit, putting J. Edgar Hoover, a young bureaucrat from the Federal Bureau of Investigation (FBI), at its head. Palmer set out to scour Bolsheviks and socialists from the country. In late 1919 and early 1920, thousands of individuals were rounded up and imprisoned on suspicion of sedition and conspiracy. Instead of obtaining arrest warrants, the authorities simply raided meeting halls and private homes, hauling in foreigners as suspected communists and spies without cause or evidence.

President Wilson quietly approved these actions, although Secretary of Labor Louis Post successfully opposed Palmer and managed to block jail terms and deportation orders. The postwar hysteria eventually died down, and most of the individuals arrested were freed. However, 249 suspects were forced aboard the USS *Buford* and deported to Finland.[4] One of the major events in FBI history, the Palmer Raids influenced the bureau's policies and procedures to the present day, as described by an FBI web page in 2015:

> The "Palmer Raids" were certainly not a bright spot for the young Bureau. But it did gain valuable experience in terrorism investigations and intelligence work and learn important lessons about the need to protect civil liberties and constitutional rights.[5]

Attorney General
A. Mitchell Palmer

ART, CULTURE, AND MIGRATION

The effects of the war were not limited to the economy or politics. The conflict brought about important changes in American arts and culture. Several leading writers had direct encounters with the war and with new literary movements. Ernest Hemingway, Somerset Maugham, John Dos Passos, and the poets E. E. Cummings and Robert Service, for example, all served as ambulance drivers in Europe.

The postwar boom also gave rise to personal mobility on a massive scale. As the demand for factory labor grew in the North, hard economic times prevailed for black farmers and sharecroppers in the South. Faced with legal efforts to prevent African Americans from voting and Jim Crow policies that separated the races, approximately 500,000 black families moved to northern cities during and after the war years, spurred by the promise of better paying jobs.[6]

The population shift had its strongest effect in industrial cities such as Cleveland, Ohio; Chicago, Illinois; Detroit, Michigan; and New York, New York. Letters sent home from the North, in addition to coverage in the *Chicago Defender* and other African-American newspapers, boosted the popular notion of the North as a promised land. In dire need of hands, some companies offered bonuses to new workers who would relocate. The Pennsylvania Railroad, for example, offered free passes to 12,000 recruits from the South.[7] This practice

ERNEST HEMINGWAY

1899–1961

Eager to reach the front and experience the dangers and glory of war, Ernest Hemingway signed up as an ambulance driver and shipped to Europe in May 1918. While serving on the Italian front, he was seriously wounded by a mortar round.

The war and his injuries changed Hemingway. After returning home, he quickly grew restless in his sedate, middle-class hometown of Oak Park, Illinois. A short experience of Europe, even in wartime, piqued his interest in new movements in art and literature. Although he had only brief experience as a reporter, he accepted a job as a foreign correspondent for the *Toronto Star* and returned to Europe in 1921.

The mass killing and destruction on the western front had robbed many people of their belief in the possibility of a better future world. Hemingway stripped his novels and short stories of old-fashioned sentiment and idealism. Hemingway's writing stood in stark contrast to that of older American writers, whose stories were written in a delicate, meandering Victorian style. The war had made Hemingway and other writers into clear-eyed realists and changed literary themes and style on both sides of the Atlantic.

THE WAR LIVES ON

World War I veterans collected pensions from the military and could draw on disability insurance. The Veterans Administration (VA) offered vocational rehabilitation, which helped returning soldiers find and keep jobs. Although the last American World War I veteran died in 2011, the VA still pays benefits to the sons, daughters, and widows of the men who fought in Europe a century ago.

was followed by the Illinois Central Railroad as well as dozens of northern factories and steel mills.

African Americans had shared the dangers of battlefields on the western front after the United States entered the war in 1917. The Selective Service Act, passed on May 10, 1917, required all men aged 21 to 31 to register for service. By the end of the war, 367,000 African Americans had joined the US Army, which still segregated the races.[8] Blacks were still not welcome in the Marine Corps, nor could they train as military pilots.

When they returned, African-American veterans expected a full share of the rights of citizenship. But the mere appearance of black men in uniform was enough to spark riots in some cities. In other cities, black veterans were not prepared to passively accept racist treatment at the hands of the justice system.

In June 1921, the rumor of a lynching at the courthouse in Tulsa, Oklahoma, was enough to bring several African Americans out into the streets with weapons, sparking the worst race riot in the country's history. Looting and arson reduced Tulsa's Greenwood, one of the country's most prosperous black

American women built ships and worked other jobs during World War I.

neighborhoods, to rubble. The police allowed the rioting to spin out of control; they even called on local pilots to fly them above the city, where they dropped incendiary devices and took shots at random civilians in the streets.

Social mobility and economic competition after the war prompted several years of turmoil. This tension gradually faded as the economic boom of the 1920s brought a higher standard of living to families throughout the country.

DEM DEUTSCHEN VOLKE

Thousands of people gathered outside the Reichstag in Berlin to protest the Versailles treaty.

THE GERMAN
REVOLUTIONS

When the armistice of 1918 took place, German armies were still fighting on foreign soil. There had been no invasion of Germany from the east or west. The new Bolshevik government of Russia had signed a peace treaty, allowing Germany to shift its military might to the western front. But with men and resources depleted by four years of fighting, the German army had simply given up.

For many German civilians, the end of the war came as a shock. Germany deployed the largest army in the world and had the most productive economy in Europe. For four years, German newspapers had confidently predicted an ultimate victory, although civilian families knew the hardships of food rationing and suffered the arrival of dead and wounded soldiers back home from the front.

With the harsh terms of the Versailles treaty set by their enemies, German soldiers and civilians felt a powerful sense of betrayal. Germany had no say at the conference. Instead, its representatives had simply signed the document, admitting blame for starting the war and allowing the Allies to hand Germany territory—and with it German citizens—over to France, Poland, Russia, and Czechoslovakia.

For many, there could be no explanation for the defeat other than treason—a stab in the back carried out by traitors on the home front. The desire for vengeance and a return to the country's former days of strength and prosperity moved the events of the next decade.

A NEW REPUBLIC

Kaiser Wilhelm II had fled Germany in November 1918 and would spend the rest of his life in the Netherlands. The dynasty that had ruled Prussia, and then a united Germany, came to an end. But the dream of a greater German state, including ethnic Germans in Austria and what was now Czechoslovakia and Poland, survived.

The postwar German government arranged elections for January 1919. Voters would select representatives to a constituent assembly, whose task would be to

German politicians gather in Weimar to establish a new government.

write a new constitution. To carry out their work, they met in Weimar, the quiet capital of the new state of Thuringia, a place far from the battlefronts.

By the new constitution adopted in August of that year, Germany was now a republic, a nation without a king or an emperor. There would be regular elections for representatives, who would meet in the Reichstag, an ornate hall in the national capital of Berlin. To pay the reparations of 269 billion reichsmarks set by the Versailles treaty, the government would have to issue bonds. Germany made the last payment on these bonds in October 2010, more than 90 years after World War I ended.[1]

The Weimar constitution did little to calm the country's political turmoil. In many German cities, street fighting erupted among soldiers, sailors, and civilians. Leftists sympathetic to the Bolshevik revolution in Russia established the Council of People's Deputies. The Communist Party of Germany formed in December 1918. The Spartacist League, a left-wing group, demanded the establishment of a communist government aligned with the Bolsheviks.

Soldiers returning from the war found a nation in disarray. There were few jobs available to veterans, whose sacrifice seemed dishonored by the country's surrender at Versailles. Many joined right-wing paramilitary units known as the Freikorps. These uniformed militias were a constant presence in large German cities such as Berlin and Munich. The members were armed, and they often engaged in street combats with leftists. On January 15, a Berlin Freikorps unit captured Rosa Luxembourg and Karl Liebknecht, two leaders of the Spartacist League, and murdered them.

TROUBLE IN MUNICH

The new government established in Weimar was on shaky ground. There was little support for the new republic on either side of a deep political divide. Germany's military, limited by the Versailles treaty to ten divisions and 100,000

Freikorps members practice shooting their rifles.

men, did not have tanks, planes, or submarines.[2] These humiliating limits deeply angered veterans and officers. When a political faction came forward calling for Germany to renounce the Versailles treaty and restore the ancient German *Reich*, or empire, the army was listening.

Munich, the capital of the southern state of Bavaria, was a center of the political turmoil. Socialist factions had confidently proclaimed a communist government in Munich on November 7, 1918. Members of the Munich Soviet Republic, under the leadership of Kurt Eisner, marched to a local army barracks and won German soldiers over to their side.

Following the armistice, Eisner stood for election as a representative to the national assembly. After losing the election in early 1919, he prepared to announce his resignation. But on his way to make the declaration, Eisner was assassinated—prompting another violent uprising and the Communist Party's seizure of the Munich city government. This government, under the leadership of Eugen Levine, directly allied with the Russian Bolsheviks. Levine announced the seizure of private property and the arrest of political opponents, eight of whom were taken as hostages and later executed as spies.

On May 3, 1919, the Freikorps and their nationalist allies staged a coup, with street fighting and executions in Munich claiming hundreds of lives. The Freikorps captured and executed communist fighters and put Levine in front of a firing squad. The Munich Soviet Republic passed into history, but it survived as a reminder of the serious threat socialist factions could pose to the new Weimar Republic.

THE NAZIS EMERGE

The street battles between the Freikorps and the communists in Munich were only the beginning of a violent period in the city's history. New factions on both left and right sprang up, their membership swelled by the ranks of the unemployed, returning war veterans, and disaffected young people who believed the new republic held little hope for Germany.

One of the many right-wing parties to emerge was the National Socialist German Workers' Party, commonly known as the Nazi Party. Originally known as the German Workers' Party when it was established by Anton Drexler in 1919, the party allied with the Freikorps and other right-wing factions, and it strived to attract members through patriotic nationalism. The party's use of the word

FASCISM ELSEWHERE

Germany was not the only country to experience fascist, or extreme right-wing, governments in the 1930s. In Hungary, Ferenc Szalasi founded the Party of National Will in 1935. The party adopted the Arrow Cross, a symbol taken from the ancient Magyars who had settled Hungary in the 900s. Just as the German Nazis harshly criticized the Treaty of Versailles, the leaders of the Arrow Cross denounced the Treaty of Trianon, which had shrunk Hungary's borders after World War I. The Arrow Cross cooperated with the German occupation of Hungary in 1944 and then seized power in October of that year. Hungary's fascist government collapsed when the Soviet army invaded the country in 1945.

socialist was meant to attract veterans and civilians who may have otherwise joined the more powerful leftist groups.

Drexler was opposed to the Versailles treaty as well as the new German republic. He believed there was a secret international plot to weaken the German nation and Jewish bankers and businessmen were at the heart of it. Drexler and his companions in the party believed their task was to overthrow the Jewish conspirators, reestablish the ancient German Reich, and unite all ethnic Germans in a single, centralized state.

In its first year of existence, the Nazi Party counted only a few dozen members. But the enthusiasm and oratorical skills of one of its members, Adolf Hitler,

Adolf Hitler served as a soldier in World War I.

brought the group to prominence. Hitler had a way with crowds. His passionate arguments favoring a rebirth of the Reich—and his speeches against leftists, communists, and Jews—convinced many thousands to join the party in the following years.

In a manifesto written by Hitler, Drexler, and Gottfried Feder, the Nazi Party declared its 25 goals.[3] These included the cancellation of the Versailles treaty, the seizure of war profits by a new German government, and an end to democracy. In the Nazis' opinion, democracy was a weak foreign ideal imposed by the Allies, not worthy of the German people. In 1921, Hitler became chairman of the Nazi Party. The party was organized on the principle that only one man would lead, and the decisions of the führer, or leader, were final. By 1921, the Nazis were strong enough to establish their own militia, known as the *Sturmabteilung* or SA.

THE BEER HALL PUTSCH

Hitler saw himself as the leader of a revolutionary movement. His ultimate goal was to overthrow the German republic and establish a single-party state, under Nazi control, with himself as the führer. A similar party arose in Italy, promising a rebirth of the Italian nation under a single leader and strongly centralized government. Benito Mussolini, the leader of this movement, proclaimed himself *Il Duce*, or the Leader. In 1922, he led a march on the capital of Rome and overthrew the Italian government. Inspired by Mussolini's example, Hitler began planning his own coup.

In early 1923, the German economy collapsed, with inflation running rampant and the savings of millions of people wiped out. The ranks of the Nazi Party swelled as discontent with the weakness of the Weimar government reached fever pitch. Hitler believed the German army was ready to join his march on Berlin to seize power.

The attempted putsch, or coup, took place in Munich on November 8. That night, the Nazis took over a beer hall where the state's governor was giving a speech. Hitler fired a shot into the ceiling and declared himself the leader of a new government. Erich Ludendorff, a German military commander during World War I, gave his support to Hitler. But the coup failed to gain widespread support. The next morning, as Hitler and Ludendorff led a group of Nazis on a march through the city, they were blocked by the state police. A gun battle took place, killing 14 Nazis and four police officers.[4] Slightly wounded, Hitler fled the scene. Two days later, he was arrested.

Hitler was found guilty of treason and given a five-year prison sentence. It was the best outcome the party could have hoped for. Although the Nazi chairman was now behind bars and the party banned, their program drew national attention. Meanwhile, the continuing economic and social turmoil in Germany turned the majority of German citizens against their own leaders.

German police set up barricades in front of a government building on the day of the Beer Hall Putsch.

THE NAZI TRIUMPH

After his release from prison, serving only eight months, Hitler returned to the podium. While in prison, he had explained his life and his goals in *Mein Kampf,* an autobiography. Now opposed to violent revolution, Hitler believed the better way to achieve his goals was to gain the complete support of the German army and work through the democratic system established by the government he despised.

The Nazis regularly campaigned for seats in the Reichstag, or German legislature. After losing badly in several elections, they finally won a majority in 1932. The result was Hitler's appointment as chancellor in January 1933. This

SURVIVAL OF THE FASCIST IDEA

The deaths of Hitler and Mussolini during World War II did not put an end to fascist ideology. Political parties that have taken up ideas advocated by the National Socialists of Germany—including Jobbik in Hungary and the Golden Dawn in Greece—are earning votes in modern elections. These parties have a few policies in common: they favor racial purity, oppose immigration, and criticize the open borders of the European Union.

Anti-Semitism, or the hatred of Jews, has also survived into the present. Far-right parties in Europe also draw on the widespread fear of terrorism to stoke Islamophobia, or the hatred of Muslims. The roots of these movements can be traced back to the close of World War I and the failure of the Versailles treaty to enforce peace, self-determination, and democracy in Europe.

brought about the abrupt end of the Weimar government, as promised in Hitler's speeches and in the pages of *Mein Kampf*.

Out of the humiliation and ruin of World War I, a new Germany had emerged. On the night of January 30, torchlight parades took place in Berlin and other German cities to celebrate the triumph of the Nazi Party. "It is almost like a dream, a fairy tale," wrote Hitler's friend and colleague Joseph Goebbels in his diary. "The new Reich has been born. Fourteen years of work have been crowned with victory. The German revolution has begun."[5]

THE LEGACY OF WORLD WAR I

Despite the hopeful prediction of H. G. Wells, World War I did not turn out to be the war to end war. The nations of Europe were not prepared to suppress their own interests to achieve a common peace, nor were they willing to grant self-determination to colonies they ruled. Further, the harsh terms of the peace treaties written to end the conflict gave rise to bitter resentments and, eventually, radical political movements in Germany and elsewhere. While the United States attempted to withdraw from Europe's tangled affairs, European leaders set out to right the perceived wrongs of the Great War that, a generation later, would draw the world back into another global conflict.

TIMELINE

1914
World War I begins in Europe.

April 1917
President Woodrow Wilson requests a declaration of war against Germany from the US Congress.

November 11, 1918
An armistice ends the war in western Europe.

January 1919
The Allies sign the Treaty of Versailles, imposing harsh peace terms on Germany.

November 8, 1923
Adolf Hitler leads the failed Beer Hall Putsch, an attempt to overthrow Germany's government.

1925
The 1925 Geneva Protocol bans the use of chemical weapons.

1929
The Great Depression begins, plunging the world into a decade-long economic downturn.

January 1933
Adolf Hitler is appointed chancellor of Germany, and the Nazi Party comes to power.

1922
The Bolshevik government of Russia establishes the Soviet Union.

November 1920
After the election of Republican Warren G. Harding, the United States begins an era of isolation.

August 1920
The Treaty of Sevres turns Ottoman territory in the Middle East over to the British and French.

August 1919
Germany establishes a new republic after representatives write a new constitution in Weimar.

1939
World War II begins as Germany invades Poland.

1945
World War II ends, leading to the collapse of the Nazi regime.

June 1945
The United Nations is established in San Francisco at a conference of 50 nations.

2010
Germany makes the final payment on bonds issued to pay World War I reparations to the Allies.

ESSENTIAL FACTS

KEY PLAYERS

- Adolf Hitler was a German war veteran who rose to the head of the Nazi Party in 1921. After leading a failed coup attempt in 1923 against the Weimar government, Hitler was briefly jailed before rising to the post of chancellor in 1933.

- Czar Nicholas II was the ruler of Russia in 1914. He sought to avoid a large-scale mobilization at the start of World War I but was overruled by his advisers.

- Kaiser Wilhelm II was the leader of Germany. He declared war in 1914, believing his nation was under threat from France, the United Kingdom, and Russia.

- Vladimir Lenin was the leader of the Bolshevik faction of the Russian Socialist Party, which took control of Russia after the revolution of October 1917.

- Woodrow Wilson was the president of the United States. He brought the country into World War I in 1917 and led negotiations at the Versailles conference in January 1919.

KEY STATISTICS

- Total war casualties: 8.5 million battle deaths and 21.2 million wounded

- Total mobilization: 65 million

- Total cost: $208 billion; $32 billion in the United States

IMPACT ON HISTORY

World War I caused widespread damage and casualties numbering in the millions. The heavy financial costs of the war disrupted the global economy and caused widespread unemployment. Inflation took hold in Germany, where public anger at the terms of the Versailles peace treaty inspired the rise to power of Adolf Hitler and the Nazi Party. The failure of the Versailles treaty to offer independence to European colonies in Africa, the Middle East, and Asia brought decades of strife as well as lingering turmoil in the Middle East.

QUOTE

"May the German-Austrian people realize harmony from the new adjustment. The happiness of my peoples was my aim from the beginning. My warmest wishes are that an internal peace will be able to heal the wounds of this war."

—*Emperor Charles of Austria-Hungary*

GLOSSARY

ANARCHIST

A person who believes countries should not have governments.

ARMISTICE

A temporary stop of fighting by mutual agreement.

ARTILLERY

Large guns manned by a crew of operators used to shoot long distances.

BOND

A financial contract in which a government or business promises to pay regular interest to bond buyers, and redeem the bonds for their face value at a certain "maturity" date.

CIVILIAN

A person not serving in the armed forces.

COMMUNIST

Having to do with a system in which the government controls the economy and owns all property.

FRONT

An area where a battle is taking place.

HOWITZER

A short cannon that fires shells in a high curving path.

HYPERINFLATION
An uncontrolled rise in prices caused by a collapse in the value of currency.

INFANTRY
Soldiers who fight on foot; the branch of the army including these soldiers.

LYNCHING
The act of seizing and murdering a suspected criminal by a civilian mob.

PILLBOX
A small concrete structure for machine guns or other weapons.

PROPAGANDA
Information used to support a political group or point of view, or to persuade the audience to support their country's participation in a war.

RECESSION
A period of negative economic growth and, usually, low demand for goods and high unemployment.

SOCIALIST
Having to do with a system in which the economy is controlled by communities or countries, rather than by the decisions of individuals.

ADDITIONAL RESOURCES

SELECTED BIBLIOGRAPHY

Macmillan, Margaret. *Paris 1919: Six Months That Changed the World*. New York: Random, 2001. Print.

Reynolds, David. *The Long Shadow: The Legacies of the Great War in the Twentieth Century*. New York: Norton, 2014. Print.

Tooze Adam. *Deluge: The Great War, America, and the Remaking of the Global Order, 1916–1931*. New York: Viking, 2014. Print.

FURTHER READINGS

Bausum, Ann. *Unraveling Freedom: The Battle of Democracy on the Home Front during World War I*. Washington, DC: National Geographic, 2010. Print.

Freedman, Russell. *The War to End All Wars: World War I*. Boston: Clarion, 2010. Print.

Pratt, Mary K. *World War I*. Minneapolis: Abdo, 2014. Print.

WEBSITES

To learn more about Essential Library of World War I, visit **booklinks.abdopublishing.com**. These links are routinely monitored and updated to provide the most current information available.

PLACES TO VISIT

Imperial War Museum
Lambeth Road
London SE1 6HZ
United Kingdom
+44 20 7416 5000
http://www.iwm.org.uk/
The Imperial War Museum includes major exhibitions on World War I and other conflicts involving the United Kingdom and its colonies.

National World War I Museum
100 W. Twenty-Sixth Street
Kansas City, MO 64108
816-888-8100
https://theworldwar.org/contact-us
The museum offers photographs, exhibitions, uniforms, and artifacts from the war.

SOURCE NOTES

CHAPTER 1. SPRING OFFENSIVE, FALL ARMISTICE

1. "The Genesis and Deployment of the German Storm Trooper on the Western Front in the Great War." *The Western Front Association.* The Western Front Association, 24 Oct. 2008. Web. 4 Aug. 2015.

2. William R. Griffiths. *The Great War: Strategies & Tactics of the First World War.* Garden City Park, NY: Square One, 2003. Print. 144.

3. Diana Preston. *Lusitania: An Epic Tragedy.* New York: Walker, 2002. Print. 303.

4. "WWI Casualty and Death Tables." *PBS.* PBS, n.d. Web. 4 Aug. 2015.

5. Frank Freidel and Hugh Sidey. "Woodrow Wilson." *White House.* White House, 2006. Web. 4 Aug. 2015.

6. "Treaty of Versailles, 1919." *United States Holocaust Memorial Museum.* United States Holocaust Memorial Museum, 20 June 2014. Web. 4 Aug. 2015.

7. Eliot Asinof. *1919: America's Loss of Innocence.* New York: D. I. Fine, 1990. Print. 86.

8. "Treaty of Versailles, 1919." *United States Holocaust Memorial Museum.* United States Holocaust Memorial Museum, 20 June 2014. Web. 4 Aug. 2015.

9. "WWI Casualty and Death Tables." *PBS.* PBS, n.d. Web. 4 Aug. 2015.

10. "Counting the Costs." *National Archives.* National Archives, n.d. Web. 4 Aug. 2015.

11. "The Economics of World War I." *National Bureau of Economic Research.* National Bureau of Economic Research, n.d. Web. 4 Aug. 2015.

CHAPTER 2. THE END OF EMPIRES

1. "Emperor Karl I's Abdication Proclamation, 11 November 1918." *FirstWorldWar.com.* Michael Duffy, 22 Aug. 2009. Web. 4 Aug. 2015.

2. R. G. Grant. *World War I: The Definitive Visual History: From Sarajevo to Versailles.* New York: DK, 2014. Print. 116–117.

CHAPTER 3. HIGH-TECH WARFARE

1. "No Survivors – Famous Regiments That Were Completely Wiped Out." *Military History Now.* militaryhistorynow.com, 21 Apr. 2015. Web. 4 Aug. 2015.

2. Spencer C. Tucker and Priscilla Mary Roberts, eds. *Encyclopedia of World War I: A Political, Social, and Military History.* Santa Barbara, CA: ABC-CLIO, 2005. Print. 452.

3. R. G. Grant. *World War I: The Definitive Visual History: From Sarajevo to Versailles.* New York: DK, 2014. Print. 42.

4. Ian V. Hogg. *Historical Dictionary of World War I.* Lanham, MD: Scarecrow, 1998. Print. xxxvii.

5. Eric A. Croddy and James J. Wirtz, eds. *Weapons of Mass Destruction: An Encyclopedia of Worldwide Policy, Technology and History.* Santa Barbara, CA: ABC-CLIO, 2004. Print. 327–328.

6. "Early Flight Decks." *Aerotoons.* G. S. Roberts, Feb. 2012. Web. 4 Aug. 2015.

7. Gerard J. Fitzgerald. "Chemical Warfare and Medical Response during World War I." *PubMed Central.* National Center for Biotechnology Information, Apr. 2008. Web. 4 Aug. 2015.

8. Ibid.

9. R. G. Grant. *World War I: The Definitive Visual History: From Sarajevo to Versailles.* New York: DK, 2014. Print. 105

10. "Weapons of War: Tanks." *FirstWorldWar.com.* Michael Duffy, 22 Aug. 2009. Web. 4 Aug. 2015.

11. Ibid.

12. Ibid.

SOURCE NOTES
CONTINUED

CHAPTER 4. ECONOMIC BUSTS AND BOOMS

1. Molly Billings. "The Influenza Pandemic of 1918." *Stanford University*. Stanford University, Feb. 2005. Web. 4 Aug. 2015.

2. Spencer C. Tucker, ed. *World War I: The Definitive Encyclopedia and Document Collection*. Santa Barbara, CA: ABC-CLIO, 2014. Print. 770.

3. "The Economics of World War I." *National Bureau of Economic Research*. National Bureau of Economic Research, n.d. Web. 4 Aug. 2015.

4. "The Immigration Act of 1924 (The Johnson-Reed Act)." *US Department of State, Office of the Historian*. US Department of State, n.d. Web. 4 Aug. 2015.

5. Steve Forbes. "The Economic Consequences of World War I – We Still Suffer from Them." *Forbes*. Forbes, 2 Aug. 2014. Web. 4 Aug. 2015.

6. "WWI Casualty and Death Tables." *PBS*. PBS, n.d. Web. 4 Aug. 2015.

7. George J. W. Goodman. "The German Hyperinflation, 1923." *Commanding Heights*. PBS, n.d. Web. 4 Aug. 2015.

8. "Germany's Hyperinflation-Phobia." *The Economist*. The Economist Newspaper Limited, 15 Nov. 2013. Web. 4 Aug. 2015.

9. Charles P. Kindleberger. *A Financial History of Western Europe*. London: Routledge, 2015. Print. 326.

10. "German Coins and Currency." *Joel Anderson: Interesting World Coins and Paper Money*. Joel Anderson, n.d. Web. 4 Aug. 2015.

CHAPTER 5. CHANGES IN THE GLOBAL MAP

1. Wess Mitchell. "Lessons to be Learned from the Collapse of the Austro-Hungarian Empire." *Budapest Times*. Budapest Times, 18 Feb. 2008. Web. 4 Aug. 2015.

2. David Reynolds. *The Long Shadow: The Legacies of the Great War in the Twentieth Century*. New York: Norton, 2013. Print. 113.

CHAPTER 6. THE LEAGUE OF NATIONS

1. "A War to End All War." *Vision*. Vision.org, Spring 2014. Web. 4 Aug. 2015.

2. "President Woodrow Wilson's Fourteen Points." *Yale Law School*. Lillian Goldman Law Library, n.d. Web. 4 Aug. 2015.

3. "Henry Cabot Lodge on the League of Nations, 12 August 1919." *FirstWorldWar.com*. Michael Duffy, 22 Aug. 2009. Web. 4 Aug. 2015.

4. "History of the United Nations." *United Nations*. United Nations, n.d. Web. 4 Aug. 2015.

CHAPTER 7. TURMOIL IN THE UNITED STATES

1. "The Deadly Virus: The Influenza Epidemic of 1918." *National Archives*. US National Archives and Records Administration, n.d. Web. 4 Aug. 2015.

2. David A. Shannon. *America between the Wars: America, 1919–1941*. Boston: Houghton Mifflin, 1979. Print. 33.

3. A. Mitchell Palmer. "The Case against the 'Reds.'" *Marxist Internet Archive*. Marxist Internet Archive, n.d. Web. 4 Aug. 2015.

4. Regin Schmidt. *Red Scare: FBI and the Origins of Anticommunism in the United States, 1919–1943*. Copenhagen, Denmark: Museum Tusculanum P, U of Copenhagen, 2000. Print. 27.

5. "A Byte out of History: The Palmer Raids." *FBI*. FBI, 28 Dec. 2007. Web. 4 Aug. 2015.

6. Chad Williams. "African Americans and World War I." *Africana Age*. Schomburg Center for Research in Black Culture, n.d. Web. 4 Aug. 2015.

7. "The Great Migration (1915–1960)." *BlackPast.org*. BlackPast.org, n.d. Web. 4 Aug. 2015.

8. "World War I and the Great Migration." *History, Art & Archives*. US House of Representatives, n.d. Web. 4 Aug. 2015.

CHAPTER 8. THE GERMAN REVOLUTIONS

1. David Crossland. "Legacy of Versailles: Germany Closes Book on World War I with Final Reparations Payment." *Spiegel Online*. Der Spiegel, 28 Sep. 2010. Web. 4 Aug. 2015.

2. "The Versailles Treaty June 28, 1919: Part V." *Yale Law School*. Lillian Goldman Law Library, n.d. Web. 5 Oct. 2015.

3. "Nazi Party Platform." *United States Holocaust Memorial Museum*. United States Holocaust Memorial Museum, n.d. Web. 4 Aug. 2015.

4. Ian Kershaw. *Hitler: A Biography*. New York: Norton, 2008. Print. 207–211.

5. William L. Shirer. *The Rise and Fall of the Third Reich*. New York: Simon & Schuster, 1990. Print. 9.

INDEX

ABOUT THE AUTHOR

Tom Streissguth has worked as a journalist, teacher, law clerk, courier, and book editor, and he has published more than 100 works of nonfiction for Enslow, Facts on File, Lerner, Greenhaven, Rosen, and other school and library publishers. A graduate of Yale University, he is the founder of The Archive, an independent publisher of historical journalism collections used by teachers, students, and researchers. He currently lives in Woodbury, Minnesota.